Segovia

Text by: César Justel
Photographs by: José Barea

EDICIONES
Aldeasa

Segovia

◄ Fountain of San Martín in the plaza of the same name.

The stone nave

The old plazas (squares) of Azoguejo, Capuchins, and Corpus; the streets that bring to mind curious stories, like the one about Life and Death, the Bad Piece of Advice, the Defenseless Ones; the Shutter of Consolation, the Walk of Piety... In their stones, in the silence of dusk, in the rumor of midday, lies the soul of Segovia. Other cities, just as old and as rich in history, are only archeological sites and stagnant memories. They fizzled out at the end of the age when they had dazzled in brilliant splendor. But Segovia is more than a relic of a distant era. Segovia has always been and continues to be alive. The city lives on in the verses of Santa Teresa, of San Juan de la Cruz, of Antonio Machado... A city made up of Roman stones from the Aqueduct, Christian stones from the cathedral, convents, stately houses, crumbling walls... and above all her three crown jewels: the Aqueduct, the Alcázar (royal palace and fortress) and the cathedral. Segovia should be contemplated from the Terminillo overlook, on the other side of the Eresma on the road to Zamarramala. From here the city looks like a boat, its bow the castle, its mainmast the cathedral, and its moorings the arches of the Aqueduct.

History reverts to legend as you go back in time. It is said to have been a descendent of Noah who came and settled in

View of the Alcázar with the cathedral in the background. ▶

this place. More believable are the settlements of remote Celt Iberian races whose presence has been confirmed by the finding of crude animal sculptures. But Segovia's most significant history began with the arrival of the Romans who subjugated the tribes and built the greatest Roman structure still standing on the Peninsula today: the Aqueduct. Later evidence of Visigoth burial sites found nearby attest to the presence of Germanic tribes, which were followed by the Arabs. The lack of Muslim artifacts and the existence of one of the richest collections of Romanesque art in Europe, supports the thesis of those historians who believe that the city was abandoned after the Islamic invasion and repopulated, starting at the end of the 11th century by Christians who came down from the northern part of the Iberian Peninsula and from beyond the Pyrenees. Under the command of the son-in-law of King Alfonso VI, Raymond of Burgundy, these settlers were accompanied by the first bishop of the city's reconstituted diocese, the Frenchman Pedro of Agen. It was Raymond of Burgundy who fortified the city, rebuilding its walls on top of the Roman defenses. A phrase appearing in the *Anales Toledanos* (Toledo Annuals) stated: "The city of Segovia was for a long time barren and then populated, it was MCXXVI".

Plaza Mayor (above). ▲
Puerta de San Andrés (below).
First section of arches of the Aqueduct. ▶

Sancho IV granted the city its charter in 1293. Among all of the kings who were tied to Segovia, the most significant was Henry IV who ordered the building of the Parral Monastery, the palace that was later the monastery of San Antonio el Real, and the remodeling of the Alcázar. He also lifted taxes on the Thursday markets, which today are still held in the Plaza Mayor. The end of the Middle Ages was a splendid and prosperous time for Segovia for many reasons: the colonization of a large territory extending out on both sides of the Sierra de Guadarrama (Guadarrama Mountains), the absorption of an important Hebrew community (which would later be relegated to the Jewish Quarter), and the creation of a powerful textile industry that would last for centuries. The primary source of the city's wealth was migrating livestock, a testament to which can be seen in the enormous monument of a shepherd with dogs and sheep located at the entrance to the city. Some of the city's houses still conserve the galleries where wool was laid out to dry. Architecturally, if the Romanesque period saw the building of churches, then the Gothic movement produced monasteries and convents. During the rule of the Trastámaras, Segovia served as the royal court, and on the 13th of December, 1474, the people of Segovia declared Isabella the Catholic to be Queen of Castile.

The wealth of the city, especially during the 15th and 16th centuries, led to the construction of luxurious palaces each with its coat of arms and adorned with Renaissance gardens. The downfall of the Castilian cities in the Revolt of the Comuneros – in which the Segovian Militia, led by Juan Bravo, played a major role – in addition to the discovery of America – which shifted poorer groups of people towards the south – were the principal causes for the beginning of Segovia's decline, despite the attention lavished on the city by the Bourbons, who founded the Reales Sitios de La Granja and Riofrío in the surrounding areas.

The 19th century saw the French occupation and the Carlist Civil Wars, which both punished Segovia and helped it to fall into anonymity, which is one of the reasons why the city has survived until today with relatively few changes.

Plaza Mayor from the cathedral tower. ▶

The Aqueduct

The first thing that visitors see upon arriving to Segovia is the Aqueduct, the greatest structure built by the Romans in Spain. It is a living lesson on art and history and how to go about studying, respecting, and above all, enjoying it.

Aqueduct and the plaza del Azoguejo. ▶

This is the only Castilian city where a Roman monument can be found in its complete form. Made of berroquena stones, the ashlars were assembled without mortar or ties. The Aqueduct, with its 158 arches, is the oldest and most impressive testimony to the history of Segovia, having remained standing through it all. The Moorish King Al Mamún attempted to destroy the Aqueduct, but his men were only able to take apart 36 of the arches and finally gave up in their attempts. Alfonso VI used some of its stones to raise the city walls, while the Catholic Monarchs Isabella and Ferdinand reconstructed it, and in the 19th century a small fort was built in its upper reaches.

The actual date of the Aqueduct's construction has always been considered a mystery although it was thought to have been during the 1st century AD, sometime between the reigns of the Emperors Domiciano, Nerva, and Trajano. At the end of the 20th century, a German archeologist managed to decipher the text on the dedication plaque by studying the anchors that held the now missing bronze letters in

Aqueduct. ▲

Casa del Agua. ▶

Calle Teodosio el Grande, next to the Aqueduct. ▶▶

place. Using this method, he was able to determine that in actuality it was the Emperor Domiciano who ordered its construction. The Aqueduct was "in use" until the 19th century. It was subjected to an intense restoration process between 1992 and 1994 due to its deteriorated state brought on by the elements and contamination; not forgetting the fact that it is located in the very center of the city of Segovia. It took its water from a subterranean tunnel coming from the Riofrío River, about 16 kilometers away. Looking closely, you can still see the tiny holes where hooks were inserted into the great stones and used to move them into position.

The Aqueduct was the result of enormous effort and sacrifice by those who built it, and the product of the willpower and knowledge of those who called for its construction. Not to mention, it was also the subject of popular lore. According to this legend, the Devil, in love with a beautiful young woman who fetched water every day from a spring, offered to build the Aqueduct in just one night in exchange for her soul. Luckily for her, the Virgin interceded in his plan and brought an early dawn surprising Maligno before he had time to place the very last stone. The young woman's soul was saved and at the same time she was set free from her daily toil of fetching water from the spring. Because of this, and similar to other cyclopic constructions whose origins can be explained by legend, the Aqueduct is also known as the "Devil's Bridge". Supposedly, each of the tiny holes left in the stones represent the dents made by the Devil's fingers as he picked them up. In front of the Aqueduct, there is a statue, a replica of the *Loba del Capitolio* suckling Romulus and Remus, given to Segovia by the city of Rome in exchange for a stone from the Aqueduct.

Plaza del Azoguejo. ▶

The cathedral

While the Aqueduct represents the Pagan world, the cathedral represents the Christian one. Dedicated to Nuestra Señora de la Asunción and San Frutos, the patron saint of Segovia, it was the last Gothic structure built in Spain.

Cathedral from the Pinarillo hillside. ▶

The city of Segovia has had three different cathedrals. The first, on the bank of the Eresma River, was destroyed by the Arians in 516. The second, built in the time of Alfonso VII in the plaza of the Alcázar, was almost completely destroyed during the Revolt of the Comuneros. It is said that the people of Segovia worked for free on the construction of the third and current cathedral, which was built between the 16th and 18th centuries, tearing down many of the houses in the Jewish Quarter to make way for it, under the direction of Juan and Rodrigo Gil of Hontañón. Consecrated in 1618, the main façade – the Puerta del Perdón (Gate of Pardon) – is adorned with a likeness of the Virgin Mary by Juan Guas; while the other two doors depict San Frutos, patron saint of Segovia, and San Geroteo, the city's first bishop.

Inside the cathedral, there are twenty chapels containing important paintings and sculptures. Some of the most outstanding examples are the reclining Christ by Gregorio Fernández, the *Retablo de la Piedad* (Altar of Piety) by Juan

Stained glass windows. ▲
Image of San Frutos. ▶
The cathedral's cloister. ▶▶

de Juni, the Romanesque Stations of the Cross and the Cristo de Pereira. The High Altar was commissioned by Charles III with a black and white marble altar piece featuring the images of San Frutos and San Geroteo. Its center is adorned with a Romanesque image of the Virgen de la Paz, donated by Henry IV.

The entrance to the tower lies in the San Blas chapel. Eighty-eight meters tall, this was the tallest tower in Spain until a bolt of lightning destroyed its upper part. The Cathedral Museum features collections of tapestries, sculptures, and paintings, as well as the sepulcher of the Prince Pedro, son of Henry II, who died at the age of twelve after falling out a window of the Alcázar. The archive, one of the most important in Spain, has 350 codices, 529 incunabula among which stand out the *Sinodal de Aguilafuente* and another containing a portrait of Isabella the Catholic, in addition to numerous books and hymns. The cloister, built by Juan Guas at the end of the 15th century, was part of the old cathedral.

Dome and pinnacles of the cathedral (left). ▲
Sculpture in front of the Puerta del Perdón (right).
Gargoyle (below).
View of the cathedral. ▶

The Devil's Cart

It was a very common practice in Spain to attribute the building of large monuments to the Devil, as was done with the Aqueduct. Another of these curious legends has to do with the Devil's cart and the architect in charge of Segovia's cathedral. When the architect realized he was not going to finish his job on time, he made a pact with the Devil. Just before finishing, he broke the pact and Lucifer, who was furious, petrified the last shipment of ashlars. This explains why one of the cathedral's towers is much flatter than the other.

The Alcázar

Another of the most characteristic images of Segovia is the silhouette of the Alcázar. Strategically located at the confluence of the Eresma and Clamores Rivers, and set against the backdrop of blue Segovian skies, it is like the figurehead on the prow of an imaginary ship.

North façade of the Alcázar. ▶

The Alcázar was built in the 12th and 13th centuries on the site of a previous fortress that is thought to have been a Celt Iberian fort and then later a Roman castle. It had already been cited by the years 1122 and 1185 and Alfonso X the Wise brought the Court here in both 1258 and 1278. This same king ordered the renovation of the Alcázar after a fire in 1262, installing an astronomical observatory in one of its towers. It was also used as a prison for the State, and in 1775 its walls held in a large group of pirates that had been captured off the coast of Tunisia. In 1765, Charles III named the Alcázar the seat of the Royal College of Arms and Artillery, the first military academy in Spain. It continued to be used for this purpose until 1862 when a badly put out fireplace provoked a horrible fire which completely destroyed the interior decoration. Although reconstruction began immediately, it has lasted almost until the present day.

Throughout its lengthy history, the Alcázar has been witness to and protagonist in many important events. It served as the birthplace for kings and princes. It was the home of Ferdinand III the Saint, Alfonso X the Wise, John II, Henry IV, the Catholic Monarchs, Philip II... It was a place for celebrations, tournaments and even a royal wedding, the fourth

South façade of the Alcázar (above). ▲

Window in the tower of John II (below).

West façade. ▶

Royal bedchamber (above). ▲
Coffering in the Throne Room (below).
Suit of armor in the Sala del Palacio Viejo. ▶
Throne Room. ▶▶

for Philip II who married Anne of Austria in November of 1570. For this event, the king ordered reforms resulting in the Patio de Armas (Arms Courtyard) and the slate capitals which contribute so much to the building's particular exterior appearance, dotted with small turrets, towers and *ajimeces* (windows divided by columns) that look out over the cliff. This feature played a role in the most dramatic event in the building's history. In 1366, Prince Pedro the son of Henry II fell to his death from the Sala de Reyes (Hall of Kings), and as legend has it he was followed by his governess who took her life in fear punishment by the king. There is a cross carved in the stone balcony marking the exact spot.

Two moments that have especially marked the history of the Alcázar were the battles between the Comuneros and the supporters of the Emperor Charles V, and the resistance of the Alcázar's occupants – many of whom lost their lives – to the invading troops of Napoleon in 1808. Both of these events demonstrated its virtual impenetrability as a fort whose only real foe was fire. Today the Alcázar is home to the General Military Archive of Segovia.

Alcázar chapel (above). ▲

Stained glass window in the Sala de las Piñas (below).

Tower of John II. ▶

The Romanesque churches

Along with the Aqueduct, the cathedral and the Alcázar, another of Segovia's crown jewels is its large quantity of Romanesque churches. Today, only eighteen of the thirty churches that once existed in Segovia are still standing and some of these were at one point even used as temples.

Church of San Martín. ▶

Recent excavations in San Lorenzo and the Santísima Trinidad have brought to light the remains of earlier buildings on which the Romanesque foundations were laid. The bell tower of San Millán, with its horseshoe arched windows, is reminiscent of more ancient styles, although in general bell towers were erected several years after the naves. The "new" churches usually consisted of a nave with wooden ceilings, and an atrium with porticos — one of the most typical characteristics of the Segovian Romanesque style — that were used as protection from the cold winds coming off of the Guadarrama Mountains. The presence of Mudejar craftsmen in the city also influenced the type of construction that was used.

An outstanding example of these churches is San Millán. Inspired by the cathedral in Jaca, which is the largest with three naves, its caliph style brick vaults are the only ones in the city. The atrium, with its capitals that have been eroded over time, served as a gathering point for Segovia's inhabitants. It was commissioned by King Alfonso I the Battler, King of Aragon, who resided in Segovia until 1166.

Church of San Juan de los Caballeros. ▲

Church of San Millán. ▶

San Martín is without a doubt the oldest of the churches, with references made to it as early as 1103. It has a triple columned atrium, three apses and a Mudejar tower. Noteworthy are the carved capitals, not to mention the *Reclining Christ* by Gregorio Fernández and the *Saint Frances* by Pedro de Mena located in the church's interior.

Other churches include San Andrés, with its Mudejar tower and Romanesque apse, or San Nicolás, whose highlights are its apse and atrium. San Juan de los Caballeros was purchased at the beginning of the 20th century by the ceramicist Daniel Zuloaga and is currently the Zuloaga Museum. Situated near the Aqueduct are the churches of El Salvador, which was built using some of its stones, and San Justo

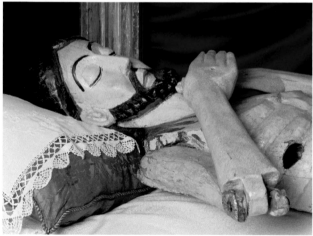

The *Cristo de los Gascones*

According to legend, this carving came from Gascony (France) where it was found buried in fear of the arrival of the Arabs. Since everyone wanted it, the carved sculpture was mounted on a blindfolded horse which was let to walk at its whim. After various stages of the journey, the horse arrived in Segovia and fell down dead at the entrance to the church of San Justo. The Gascons that had followed the animal decided to stay in the city, settling in what is still known today as the calle Gascos (street of the Gascons). The Christ is still in San Justo and since 1628 its float has participated in the procession held on Holy Friday, thereby creating the oldest image of Segovia's Holy Week celebrations.

Fresco in the church of San Justo (above). ▲
Cristo de los Gascones (below).
Church of San Nicolás. ▶

which has one of the few Romanesque tymphanum sculptures in Segovia, valuable Romanesque frescoes on its interior, and the carving of *Cristo de los Gascones*, a reclining figure from the 11th century with folded arms, about which there is a curious legend. The highlight of the Trinidad is the portico and its capitals, and San Esteban boasts a bell tower considered to be among the finest in Europe. San Lorenzo, with its three apses, is located outside the city walls in one of the most traditional areas of Segovia. Also outside the city walls on the road to Zamarramala, which was its parish for centuries, is the church of the Vera Cruz, located in an enclave with one of the best views of the city. Some say that it was built by the Templars in order to store a piece of Christ's cross, but more than likely it was built by the Knights of the Holy Sepulchre. When their order dissolved the church was passed on to the Order of Malta, who joined the church of San Juan of Jerusalem in 1531. The Knights of this order still take care of the church's upkeep and celebrate their religious ceremonies here, the most spectacular being the rituals of Holy Friday, when they participate in a nocturnal procession dressed in black habits and carrying candles. The plaque set into its entrance marks the date of the dedication of the temple: April 13th, 1208.

Church and plaza de San Lorenzo (above). ▲
Capitals of San Martín (below).
Church of the Vera Cruz. ▶

The church of the Vera Cruz

This former temple is one of the few churches with a circular floor plan still standing in Spain. The precedence for this architectural style comes from the Roman baptisteries of the first centuries of Christianity and is characteristic of the temples built by the different orders of knights that were founded during the Crusades in Palestine, imitating the Rock Mosque and the basilica of the Holy Sepulcher, both in Jerusalem. Among its most well-known features are the chapel of Lignum Crucis – where for centuries a relic of the Holy Cross was revered–, the Roman likeness in stone of the Virgen de la Paz, a crucifix from the 18th century and the central tabernacle where knights kept a vigil over their weapons before their appointment.

Convents and monasteries

Kings and Saints left the imprint of their monastic foundations in Segovia, many of which still survive today. While not all of them conserve their original functions, they still make up one of the most interesting groups of Segovian monuments.

Patio of the Parral Monastery. ▶

Domingo de Guzmán founded the convent of Santa Cruz la Real in the 18th century, the first Dominican order in Spain. Located next to the cave on the banks of the Eresma where the Saint would go to do penance, the current building, with its magnificent Elizabethan entrance, was built in the 15th century under the patronage of the Catholic Monarchs. The regretfully famous Tomás de Torquemada, who later became the Great Inquisitor of the Holy Office and the prosecutor of Jews and converts, was once a prior here, and it is said to be the site of one of the ecstasies of Saint Teresa de Jesús. The monastery was later a home for the elderly and today is a private university.

The memory of San Juan de la Cruz is kept alive in the convent of the Discalced Carmelites next to the Fuencisla Sanctuary, where he lived, died and is buried. The convent of Corpus Christi is in the building that long ago housed the Sinagoga Mayor (High Synagogue) in the Jewish Quarter. Some of the convents that have lost their monastic functions are that of San Francisco, with its interesting Elizabethan cloister, which is now the seat of the Artillery Academy, or that of the Capuchins, from the 17th century, which has been occupied by Oblate nuns since 1996.

Hieronymite Monk. Parral Monastery (above). ▲
Coffering in the convent of San Antonio el Real (below).
Door of the convent of Santa Cruz la Real. ▶

But the best of all – and perhaps the least well known – is that of San Antonio el Real, whose collection of Mudejar coffering is among the most important in Spain. In addition, the church houses the *Calvario de Bruselas*, a sculpted altarpiece from the 15th century that tells the story of the Passion of Christ.

The principal Segovian monastery is without a doubt the Parral, a Gothic building from the 15th century. Located next the Eresma River in one of the most beautiful spots in Segovia, this National Monument contains various examples of Gothic, Mudejar, and Plateresque cloisters. Once again inhabited by Hieronymite monks, it has a beautiful exterior façade and an interesting altarpiece on the High Altar. Not far from here is San Vicente el Real, built on the place where there was once a Temple honoring Jupiter.

Old convent of Capuchins. ▲

Parral Monastery. ▶

Grand houses and palaces

Houses of canons, nobles, and Jews... All of the Medieval Segovian social stratums have left their mark on the wide selection of civil architecture that makes up one of the main points of interest in the city.

Puerta de la Claustra. ▶

The Canonjías (Canonry) district, which in the Middle Ages was a walled-in area inhabited by the canons of the cathedral, had four gates of which only one survives, the Puerta de la Claustra (the Cloister Gate). On calle Daoíz and the parallel calle Velarde, there are still a few houses which have preserved their ancient Romanesque entrances. Among the mansions belonging to nobility, the most famous is the 15th century Casa de los Picos (House of the Points) which is used today as an exposition space, and whose name comes from the diamond points on its façade: 365 in total, one for every day of the year. It is said to have belonged to an incredibly wealthy Arab who was forced to leave after the expulsion decree of the Catholic Monarchs in 1492. Although still sometimes referred to as the "House of the Moor", the next owner covered it with stone points in order to give it a new name. Other grand houses are those that once belonged to the Marquis of Lozoya, with its beautiful Romanesque entrance; the Italian inspired palace of the Count of Alpuente; the 16th century house of

Patio of the palace of the Count of Alpuente. ▲

Window of the palace of the Count of Alpuente. ▶

Casa de los Picos. ▶▶

The Casa de los Picos

One of the many legends surrounding the Casa de los Picos makes the owner out to be a certain Íñigo de la Hoz who, while fighting against the Arabs, captured and tortured an important man. Once back in Segovia he dedicated himself to raising his only daughter, Guiomar, who claimed to have been impregnated by a youth who climbed over the walls of the house. On hearing this, her father ordered points to be placed on the walls to prevent the youth from returning. Before fleeing the young man revealed that it had been an act of revenge as he was the son of the Arab that Don Íñigo had tortured. According to another legend, there is a hidden treasure inside one of the points.

the Marquis of Moya – better known as the Casa de las Cadenas (House of Chains); the palace of Quintanar, with its original entrance surrounded by helmets and an enormous shield held in place by two savages; the palace of Ayala Berganza, which has been converted into a luxury hotel; and the Baroque and Plateresque Episcopal Palace. In addition, there are a number of towers that evoke the city's warring past such as the Arias Dávila decorated with sgraffitos, the tower of Hércules, which is integrated into the Dominican convent of Santo Domingo de Guzmán, or the 15th and 16th century Torreón de Lozoya that is used today as an exposition space.

Casa de las Cadenas. ▲
Door to the palace of the Count of Cheste. ▶
Torreón de Lozoya and church of San Martín (above). ▶▶
Door to the palace of Quintanar (left).
Windows of the palace of Ayala Berganza (right).

The Calle Real

The main artery of the old city runs between two largest plazas in Segovia – Azoguejo and Mayor – and despite the multiple names that it bears today, it continues to honor the memory of its old designation as the Calle Real.

Mirador de la Canaleja. ▶

Everything in Segovia begins at the foot of the Aqueduct in the plaza del Azoguejo meaning the "small zoco" or small Arab marketplace, due to the fact that it has always been the site of the market. In and around the plaza there are taverns, restaurants, and bars among other things. There are many streets leading away from Azoguejo, with the most important being the Calle Real. Known in olden days as calle Cintería (Ribbon), this name was given in accordance with the medieval custom of naming streets after the things sold on them, in this case ribbons, yarn and thread. Today the street bears three successive names: Cervantes (the old calle Real del Carmen named for the convent that is no longer standing), Juan Bravo, and Isabel la Católica, before finally ending in Segovia's other great plaza, the Plaza Mayor.

At the beginning of the Calle Real, lies the Mirador de la Canaleja (Canaleja Outlook), with views of the San Millán district and, in the background, the mountain of the Mujer Muerta (Dead Woman). Located in front of this is the Cervantes Theater and the Casa de los Picos, while next to it is the virtually unknown 16th century Casa de los del Río. It then makes its way to the small Platero Oquendo square, which houses the late 15th century palace of the Count of Alpuente. On a tiny side street is the Alhóndiga building

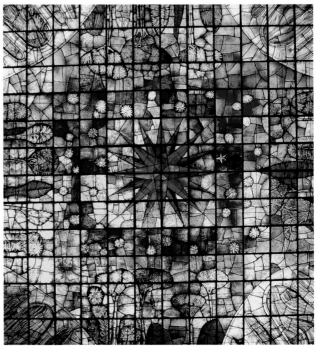

Plaza Mayor (above). ▲
Palace of the Count of Alpuente (below).
Plaza Mayor and City Hall. ▶

that was once used for storing grains and now houses the Municipal Archives.

Halfway down the street at the entrance to the plaza of Medina del Campo and next to the Romanesque church of San Martín, is the statue of Juan Bravo, the Comunero who lost his life standing up to the troops of the Emperor Charles V. There are a number of grand houses looking out over the plaza such as the Torreón de los Lozoya and the house known either as the Casa de Juan Bravo or as the home of the Mexía Tovar family. On its raised side, the plaza is graced by the 16th century building known as the "Hospital de Viejos" (Elderly Hospital). Once part of Henry IV's old palace, it is now the Esteban Vicente Museum of Contemporary Art.

Proceeding along the Calle Real, on the right is the Cárcel Vieja (Old Jail), now the Public Library with the Habsburg coat of arms on the façade. Further along is the small square of the Corpus and the convent of the same name, and finally the Plaza Mayor, with the music kiosk in the center.

Esteban Vicente Contemporary Art Museum. ▲
Church of San Martín. ▶
Casa de los del Río (above). ▶▶
Statue of Juan Bravo (below).

The Revolt of the Comuneros

In 1520 the most important families in Segovia embraced the Comunero cause against the Emperor Charles V, believing that his absolute monarchy sought to weaken the powers given to the Castilian cities. One of the most emblematic Segovian figures in this uprising was Juan Bravo, who ordered the hanging of the official Rodrigo de Tordesillas who voted in favor of the king in the legislative body in Santiago de Compostela. After a series of battles, the Flemish cardinal Adrian of Utrecht — later to become Pope Adrian VI — who had been named regent by the king, finally defeated the Comuneros in Villalar, and ordered the execution of their principal leaders: Juan Bravo of Segovia, Juan de Padilla of Toledo, and Francisco Maldonado of Salamanca. The coat of arms of Segovia bears a likeness of the Aqueduct and the head of Juan Bravo.

The Jewish Quarter

The Jewish Quarter is located with its back to the Alcázar. Its noble mansions are a testament to Segovia's powerful Hebrew community that was a model of peaceful coexistence for over two-hundred years until the Jews were expelled from the Iberian Peninsula in 1492.

View of the Jewish Quarter from the cathedral tower. ▶

The first Jewish settlers probably arrived in Segovia at the end of the 6th century. In 1391 the persecution of Jews began both here, and in other cities all over Spain. In 1412 the Arab and Jewish communities were forced to move to certain areas of the city, although shortly afterwards they spread out into other areas of Segovia. The Jewish Quarter was understood to be the area from the Sinagoga Mayor to the old slaughterhouse (today the Casa del Sol) and the puerta de San Andrés. In 1480 the Catholic Monarchs limited Jews to the area encompassing the Jewish Quarter, and in 1492 they were permanently expelled from Spain.

At one point, Segovia had up to seven synagogues, the most important being the Sinagoga Mayor, which was converted into the church of Corpus Christi in 1419. It was destroyed by a fire in 1899, but the plasterwork on the capitals and the arches have been restored to their original state. It is made up of three naves divided by horseshoe arches and octagonal pillars with large plaster capitals. Today it belongs to a community of nuns from the Order of Saint Clare and contains other interesting features such as the *miqwab* (ceremonial pool), which is hidden behind one of its walls. The surrounding area includes some well preserved old houses made of masonry, brick, and wood, which

Jewish Quarter. ▶
Capital of the church of Corpus Christi (above). ▼
Church of Corpus Christi, old Sinagoga Mayor (below).

were covered in sgraffitos in the 19th century and have now been restored to their original appearance.

The grandest of these houses once belonged to important members of the Jewish community such as the house-palace of Abraham Senneor, on calle de la Judería Vieja, which is today the Didactic Center for the Jewish Quarter. Senneor was high judge of the Jewish communities of Castile, and his descendants were related to the Comunero Juan Bravo. On calle de San Geroteo, behind the cathedral, built over part of the Jewish Quarter, the Madres Jesuitinas primary school occupies the place where the Sinagoga Nueva (New Synagogue) once stood. The new synagogue was built to substitute the old Sinagoga Mayor when it was converted into the church of Corpus Christi in 1419. At the edge of the district and built over a spur of rock jutting into the Valley of Clamores, is the Casa del Sol (House of the Sun), the old slaughterhouse of the Jewish Quarter which today houses the Museum of Segovia.

Leaving the walled district through the gate of San Andrés (over which there is a Wall Information Center), the path crosses through the valley of Clamores and arrives at the Pinarillo hillside, site of the old Jewish cemetery where tombs are preserved in both natural and anthropomorphic caves of which many are still intact.

Didactic Center for the Jewish Quarter (above). ▲
Puerta de San Andrés and cathedral (below).
Old Jewish cemetery. ▶

Routes outside the city walls

Outside its walls, the city is bordered by two paths that run parallel to the two Segovian rivers: the Eresma and the Clamores. Used by Segovians as recreational spaces, these two areas also serve as excellent locations from which to enjoy the most spectacular views of the city's monuments.

San Marcos meadow and Alcázar. ▶

The path known as Santo Domingo de Guzmán runs along the Eresma, where the ancient Dominican monastery of Santa Cruz la Real rises up next to it. The other side of the river gives way to the beautiful path of the Alameda, whose elms had to be cut down due to Dutch elm disease. The Alameda was Segovia's first park and can be traced back to the middle of the 16th century. Around it are the monasteries of San Vicente and Parral, and the Casa de la Moneda, which is located next to the dam with its spectacular falling water.

Downstream is the church of San Marcos and the beautiful private garden of El Romeral, the work of Leandro Silva who was also responsible for the restoration of the Botanical Garden in Madrid. And a bit farther along lies the curious church of Vera Cruz, where the Knights of the Order of the Holy Sepulcher held vigil over their weapons. When this order dissolved it became the Orden de Malta who are the current stewards of this church. The most beautiful views of the city can be seen from here on the road to Zamarramala, shielded by the Sierra de Guadarrama in the background. The sanctuary of Nuestra Señora de la Fuencisla lies very close at the foot of the cliff known as Peñas Grajeras. It is known for its image of the Patron Saint of Segovia, although

The Virgen de la Fuencisla
The name Fuencisla "flowing fountain" refers to the place where the image of the virgin was found. According to legend, a Jewess converted to Christianity was punished by her own people and condemned to be thrown off the cliff of Peñas Grajeras; she commended herself to the Virgen de la Fuencisla and made it to the bottom unharmed. She was baptized as María, although the people called her María del Salto (María of the Jump). This miracle is referred to in a medieval poem sung in the time of Alfonso X the Wise, and a hermitage was built to give the image a home. The current sanctuary was built in the late 16th century and ever since the image has been carried in procession to the cathedral once a year where it remains for ten days.

Arco de la Fuencisla (left). ▲
Virgen de la Fuencisla (right).
The Alcázar reflected in the water of the Eresma. ▶

it is said that the first primitive image was hidden in the old church of San Gil on the banks of the Eresma during the arrival of the Arabs, and not found again until the reign of Alfonso VII, at which time it was taken to the old cathedral and placed on its façade.

Next to the sanctuary is the Carmelite convent wherein lie the remains of Saint John of the Cross, although some of the Saint's relics are divided among other churches, convents, and sanctuaries.

The second path begins at the Sancti-Spiritu bridge in the popular San Millán district that was once the old Moorish Quarter. Crossing calle de Ezequiel González, whose trees have recently been cut down with the exception of a one hundred year old elm, the path turns into the Cuesta de los Hoyos. To the left is the Pinarillo hillside and the old Jewish cemetery, and to the right is an extensive area wooded by poplars, willows and elders and backed up by the city wall. This beautiful path ends at the foot of the Alcázar and joins the San Marcos meadow where the two routes and the two rivers meet.

The Alcázar from the Vera Cruz. ▲

Parral Monastery. Sepulcher of Juan Pacheco. ▶

Convent of the Discalced Carmelites. ▶▶

Around Segovia

Winds from the Guadarrama, green pine forests of La Granja and Valsaín, mayoresses of Zamarrama-la, fragrant resins from Coca, whiskey from Palazuelo (the first whisky produced in Spain)... This is the Castile of the flat horizons and solemn sunsets.

Palace of La Granja. ▶

The Royal Sites

The Real Sitio de La Granja de San Ildefonso is located only eleven kilometers from Segovia. King Henry IV built a hermitage here for San Ildefonso in the middle of the 15th century. The Catholic Monarchs gave the hermitage to the Hieronymite monks of Parral who built the guesthouse that was the origin of La Granja. The first Bourbon king, Philip V, bought the land from the monks in the 18th century and ordered the building of the palace that is here today, and which served as a royal residence until the 19th century. Currently the palace is a museum, and its rooms can be visited as well as its gardens which occupy more then six square kilometers and are elaborately decorated with fountains, statues, and waterfalls, in imitation of the ones in Versailles. The grand avenues in front of the palace are flanked by hundred year old trees, among which there is a sequoia known as "the King". The Real Fábrica de Cristales de la Granja (The Royal Glass Factory) is very close to the palace, and in addition to the factory it contains a Museo del Vidrio (Glass Museum). After the death of her husband, the wife of Philip V, Isabel de Farnesio, ordered the construction of another palace only fifteen kilometers from La Granja and seven kilometers away from Segovia. The Real Sitio of Riofrío had churches, barracks, a theater and official housing. It is surrounded by an enormous oak wood full of grazing deer, and a Hunting Museum.

The Romanesque route and the route of the roasted lamb

The town of Sotosalbos is located only eighteen kilometers from Segovia on the highway to Soria. The beautiful Romanesque church of San Miguel is located here, and like all Segovian Romanesque churches it has a simple layout, with a rectangular nave ending in the east in a rectangular apse. A portico runs along the southern wall and there is a bell tower on the wall to the north of the apse. The interior decoration is lavish and rich. Between the corbels on the cornices of the portico there are scenes depicting warriors in combat and minstrels playing instruments. The capitals in the atrium depict mermaid-like creatures with the heads of women and the bodies of birds. The capital representing the Adoration of the Magi, a topic very characteristic to the 13th century, especially stands out, as do the 14th century arches that flank the atrium gate. The Virgen de la Sierra is ven-

Staircase in the palace of Riofrío (above). ▲
Reliefs on the church of Sotosalbos (below).
Church of Sotosalbos. ▶

erated in this church. The late 13th century Romanesque sculpture of the sitting Virgin with baby Jesus came from the Cistercian abbey of Nuestra Señora de la Sierra, whose ruins can be visited just four kilometers away. In addition, the church contains four panels from the middle of the 15th century that must have formed part of a primitive altarpiece and that represent two cardinal virtues and two prophets. The town of Sotosalbos was very wealthy and of great importance in raising livestock due to its abundant pastures. Even today the village is not only famous for its church, but also for its restaurants specializing in roasted lamb, which attract visitors from far and wide.

The fortress protecting the town of Turégano, only 16 kilometers from Sotosalbos, has been a palace, a granary and a castle successively. Its dungeons witnessed the suffering of Antonio Pérez, secretary to Philip II, who finally escaped after seducing the daughter of the jailer.

Not far from here is the town of Sepúlveda, also known as "The Lamb Coast" for the large number of restaurants and taverns that specialize in this dish. Of its fortress, famous in days gone by, there are only a few walls and a couple of towers remaining today. This castle was the site for the writing of the charter that bears its name and that served as the origin of Castilian establishments. Sepúlveda boasts three magnificent Romanesque churches, including San Salvador which is the oldest in the province.

Close to Sepúlveda are the Hoces del Río Duratón, a Natural Park with more than twenty-five kilometers of spectacular scenery. The Duratón River runs between sheer vertical walls that can reach seventy meters high, and is circled by vultures overhead. It is a place with cave-like hermitages, Visigoth burial sites, Romanesque churches such as that of San Frutos, and abundant legends.

The town of Pedraza is on the way back to Segovia. With only one entrance – the Puerta de la Villa, Moorish and rebuilt in the 16th century – it is one of the few completely walled towns in Spain. The Calle Real, running into the Plaza Mayor, is flanked by grand old houses. The Romanesque tower of the church of San Juan rises up in the porticoed Plaza Mayor, one of the most beautiful in Castile, as do the palaces of the Marquis of Lozoya and the Marquis of Miranda. But the town's most important monument is its castle. First Roman and then Arab, for five years the castle's tribute tower served as a prison for the French princes who later became Kings Francis II and Henry II. This fortress was acquired by the painter Ignacio Zuloaga and today belongs to his descendants who have converted it into a museum exhibiting the work of

Cuéllar Castle (above). ▲
Capitals of Santa María la Real de Nieva (below).
Pedraza. Puerta de la Villa. (above). ▶
Turégano (below).

this Guipuzcoan artist. Pedraza has a number of establishments serving delicious roasted lamb, thanks in part to its location on the ancient livestock route. The flocks of sheep, whose wool was exported to the rest of Europe, were the origin of the town's economic power.

Santa María la Real de Nieva, Coca and Cuéllar

On the highway running north to Valladolid lies the convent of Santa María la Real de Nieva, with one of Spain's most interesting and well-preserved cloisters illustrating the transition from Romanesque style to Gothic. The capitals depict scenes from the everyday life of its inhabitants during the Middle Ages, including well-known farm chores such as images of peasants reaping, gathering grains, harvesting grapes for wine, or slaughtering animals. Ten years ago, the remains of Queen Blanca of Navarre were found in the church. Seventeen kilometers away is the castle of Coca, with its preserved barbican, turret, and moat. The castle was symbolic of the final power of the nobility before the statist vision of the Catholic Monarchs spelled the end for dukedoms and great estates. Coca and Cuéllar, thirty kilometers apart, were longtime rivals. The castle of Cuéllar belonged to Don Beltrán de la Cueva, while that of Coca – built by the Bishop Fonseca, famous for his sumptuous banquets – supported the claim of Isabella the Catholic over that of the Beltraneja, the supposed bastard daughter of Don Beltrán. With Isabella's triumph, Coca went on to become the best conserved of all of the Segovian castles.

This castle served as a prison and it was here that Alonso de Guzmán was held after his failed attempt at proclaiming himself King of Andalusia in the middle of the 16th century. The fortress protected the surrounding town where it is said that the Roman Emperor Theodosius was born. The castle of Cuéllar, continues to be an imposing fortress with an outstanding southern facing balcony that looks out over the large pine wood surrounding the villa. The Romantic poet Espronceda was held prisoner here and wrote several of his works from its dungeons. The town still has several churches, most notably that of San Martín with its three Mudejar apses. Cuéllar claims to be the site of the oldest bullfights in Spain, celebrated for the first time here on orders from Don Beltrán de la Cueva.

Cloister of Santa María la Real de Nieva. ▶